First World War
and Army of Occupation
War Diary
France, Belgium and Germany

59 DIVISION
Divisional Troops
Royal Scots Fusiliers
6/7th Battalion Pioneers
1 February 1918 - 31 May 1918

WO95/3017/8

The Naval & Military Press Ltd
www.nmarchive.com
Published in association with The National Archives

Published by

The Naval & Military Press Ltd

Unit 10 Ridgewood Industrial Park,

Uckfield, East Sussex,

TN22 5QE England

Tel: +44 (0) 1825 749494

www.naval-military-press.com

www.nmarchive.com

This diary has been reprinted in facsimile from the original. Any imperfections are inevitably reproduced and the quality may fall short of modern type and cartographic standards.

© **Crown Copyright**
Images reproduced by permission of The National Archives, London, England, 2015.

Contents

Document type	Place/Title	Date From	Date To
Heading	WO95/3017/8		
Heading	59th Division 6-7th Bn Royal Scots Fusiliers (Pioneers) Feb-May 1918 From 15 Div 45 Bde		
Heading	6/7 Royal Scots Fusiliers (Pioneers) from 1-2-18 To 28-2-18 (Volume XXI)		
War Diary	Wanquetin	01/02/1918	04/02/1918
War Diary	Arras	05/02/1918	06/02/1918
War Diary	Wilderness Camp	07/02/1918	08/02/1918
War Diary	Arras	09/02/1918	21/02/1918
War Diary	Blairville	22/02/1918	22/02/1918
War Diary	Mory	23/02/1918	28/02/1918
Heading	59th Divisional Troops War Diary 6/7th Battalion Royal Scots Fusiliers Pioneers March 1918		
Heading	War Diary 6/7 R. Sc. Fus. (Pi.) March 1918 & A Letter from The C.O.		
Heading	War Diary 6/7 Royal Scots Fusiliers (Pioneers) From 1-3-18 To 31-3-18 (Vol XXII)		
War Diary	Mory	01/03/1918	21/03/1918
War Diary	Vraucourt	21/03/1918	23/03/1918
War Diary	Behagnies	24/03/1918	24/03/1918
War Diary	Boocquoy	24/03/1918	26/03/1918
War Diary	Bienvillers	26/03/1918	26/03/1918
War Diary	Sus-St-Leger	27/03/1918	29/03/1918
War Diary	Houdain	30/03/1918	31/03/1918
Miscellaneous	Historical Section (Military Branch),		
Map	Battle Zone		
Heading	59th Divisional Pioneers 6/7th Battalion Royal Scots Fusiliers (Pioneers) April 1918		
War Diary	Houdain	01/04/1918	01/04/1918
War Diary	Watou	02/04/1918	04/04/1918
War Diary	Middlesex Camp Ypres.	05/04/1918	20/04/1918
War Diary	Houtkerque	21/04/1918	30/04/1918
Heading	War Diary 6/7th Royal Scots Fusiliers (Pioneers) From 1-5-18 To 31-5-18 (Vol XXIV)		
War Diary	Farm L.30.a.56 (Sheet 27)	01/05/1918	05/05/1918
War Diary	Houtkerque	06/05/1918	06/05/1918
War Diary	St. Omer	07/05/1918	09/05/1918
War Diary	Rebecq	10/05/1918	10/05/1918
War Diary	Nedonchelle	11/05/1918	13/05/1918
War Diary	Estree-Cauchie	14/05/1918	18/05/1918
War Diary	Mametz	19/05/1918	31/05/1918
Miscellaneous	Headquarters	01/06/1918	01/06/1918

wo 95
3017/8

59TH DIVISION

6-7TH BN ROYAL SCOTS FUSILIERS
(PIONEERS)
FEB - MAY 1918.

From 15 DIV
45 BDE

To UK

P/59
WM 32

21st
7 shut

CONFIDENTIAL

WAR DIARY.
of
6/7 ROYAL SCOTS FUSILIERS.
(PIONEERS)

from 1-2-18 to 28-2-18

(Volume XXI.)

Army Form C. 2118.

WAR DIARY
or
INTELLIGENCE SUMMARY.
(Erase heading not required.)

Instructions regarding War Diaries and Intelligence Summaries are contained in F.S. Regs., Part II. and the Staff Manual respectively. Title pages will be prepared in manuscript.

Place	Date	Hour	Summary of Events and Information	Remarks and references to Appendices
WANQUETIN	1st Monday	8.25am	The Battalion marched out at 8.25 in the morning to take part in a Brigade Exercise. A took up a defensive position facing the village from the West & was attacked during the forenoon by the other 3 Battalions in the Brigade. When the attacking force broke through our front system our reserve company ('B' Coy) made a successful counter-attack their cover from a smoke barrage. The Battalion marched back to billets about 1.30 p.m. for dinner. In the evening 'B' Company gave a concert.	
	2nd	9-12-45	The morning was spent in company training which included digging & wiring practices. The Medical Officer showed a class for training stretcher bearers at 11am. 'D' Company & 72 men of 'A' Company moved to ARRAS to form part of a working party from the 46th Infantry Brigade who were working for the Corps H.A. Route-march route by WARLUS-DAINVILLE. Inter-Brigade Cross-country run took place in the afternoon. Four Battalions represented the 45th Brigade. The result was 46th Bde. 40 points, 44th Bde. 39 points and 45th Bde. 30 points.	
	3rd		In the morning Church Services were held. In the afternoon 'A','B','& 'C' Companies had Baths. A/Sgt (A/C.S.M.) W. Williams & Sgt R. Kerr's names appeared in orders as having been awarded the Belgian Croix de Guerre. Major Stn. Birks 5th Bn. R.I. Fus. reported to the Battalion for duty & was appointed 2nd in Command.	
	4th	9-12-30	The morning was spent in company training which included wiring practice & Box respirator drill. Everyone in the Battalion wore their Box respirators for 1/2 an hour during the day. 2/Lt E. McQuaid rejoined the Battalion from the depot Battalion. The Officers gave a concert in the evening.	
	5th	9-12-30 1-6	All morning was spent in cleaning hut equipment. In the afternoon the Battalion moved from WANQUETIN to billets at ECOLE des JEUNES FILLES, ARRAS. The Bn. left WANQUETIN at 2.30 p.m. & arrived at ARRAS about 6 p.m. No men fell out en route.	
ARRAS	6th		All day spent in billets - another inspection of feet, boots etc.	

Army Form C. 2118.

WAR DIARY
or
INTELLIGENCE SUMMARY.
(Erase heading not required.)

Instructions regarding War Diaries and Intelligence Summaries are contained in F. S. Regs., Part II. and the Staff Manual respectively. Title pages will be prepared in manuscript.

Place	Date February	Hour	Summary of Events and Information	Remarks and references to Appendices
ARRAS	6 (Contin)		At 4.15 p.m. the Battalion left the ECOLE de JEUNES FILLES & marched to WILDERNESS CAMP. They reached billets in the Camp about 5 o'clock. No men fell out on the march.	
WILDERNESS CAMP	7ª	9-12.30	The morning was spent in Company training including Physical Drill & Bayonet Practice.	
		2-4	In the afternoon the companies held cleaning parades.	
	8ª	9-12.30 2-4	All day spent in Company training.	
	9ª	9-12	The morning was spent in Company training. The M.O. gave the Jun N.C.O.s a lecture on their duties. In the afternoon the Battalion moved back to billets in GRANARY, ARRAS getting in about 5 o'clock. No men fell out on the march. Today Lieut W. R. Hutchison was granted permission to wear badge & rank of Captain pending appearance of same in the London Gazette.	
ARRAS	10ª		Church Services were held during the morning. 2 Platoons of 'A' company & 3 Officers & 3 platoons of 'B' company went out all day on a working party & 5 Officers and 200 men from 'C' were out another working party. 'D' Company rejoined the Battalion in the GRANARY billets this afternoon.	
	11ª	9-12.30	The Lewis Gun Officer started a novices class today. Lieut Thanet held a wiring class for the Officers of 'D' company. 3 Working parties were found by the Battalion today. 2 Officers & 200 men from 'B' company. 2 Officers & 150 men from 'A' company. 2 Officers & 200 men from 'C' plus 1 platoon from 'D' company. These parties were out all day digging gun positions for the 17ª Corps Heavy Artillery. Captain N.B. Duncan left the Battalion today to do duty with the Labour Corps Base Depot.	

WAR DIARY
or
INTELLIGENCE SUMMARY.

(Erase heading not required.)

Army Form C. 2118.

Instructions regarding War Diaries and Intelligence Summaries are contained in F. S. Regs., Part II. and the Staff Manual respectively. Title pages will be prepared in manuscript.

Place	Date	Hour	Summary of Events and Information	Remarks and references to Appendices
ARRAS	February 12th	9-1030	The recruits from our class paraded during the forenoon. The signalling officer worked at new class for signallers. The 3 working parties were out all day working for the 17th Corps H.A.	
		9-5		
	13th	9-12-30	The recruits from our class paraded during the morning. The working parties were out all day. At night "D" Company. The recruits 17th Corps working parties were away all day. At night "D" Company & 2 N.C.O.s per platoon attended a demonstration by Corps Chemical Adviser with Lees projector. It was 1 N.C.O. per platoon & it was not a success. A draft of 47 men arrived today.	
		9-5		
	14th	9-7.30	Signalling, Lewis Gun & Bombing classes were held today. The 3 usual working parties were out all day. In the evening "B" & "A" Companies had baths. Captain R.J. Bacon went to a Bath demonstration at L10, sheet 62 D—	
	15th	9-4	Bombing, Lewis Gun & Signalling classes were held again today. The usual working parties were out.	
	16th	9-4	All the N.C.O.s from "A" Company paraded under Lieut Shanks M.C. for wiring instruction. The Signalling & Lewis Gun classes were held as usual. The working parties for 17 Corps H.A. went out as usual except 100 men from "B" Company who went to the forward area to work. This Labour party was under Lieut Watson & took over trenches to live in, in the reserve line tonight—	
	17th		Church Services were held during the morning. Working parties were out as usual. "B" Company wiring party alike during no reserve trenches.	
	18th	9-12.30	"B" Company wiring class was during the morning. The usual working parties were out. "B" Company wiring party still did the trenches.	

WAR DIARY or INTELLIGENCE SUMMARY.

Army Form C. 2118.

Place	Date	Hour	Summary of Events and Information	Remarks and references to Appendices
ARRAS	19th February	9-4	The Lewis Gun Signalling Classes were held, & the usual working parties for 17th Corps H.A. were out. This morning 100 other ranks under Lieut J.A. Bowis kept over the trenches and wiring from the 'B' Company party. The 'B' Company wiring party rejoined the Battalion in the GRANARY tonight.	
	20th	7-2000	The whole Battalion (less 'C' wiring party) paraded in the morning the Commanding Officer addressed it on "Men overstaying leave to U.K." A new Lewis gun class started today. The signalling class was held as usual. The usual working parties were out all day. 'C' Company wiring party rejoined the Battalion in GRANARY, ARRAS at night.	
	21st	9-10, 10-30	This morning the Battalion leaves the 15th Division to go as Pioneer Battalion to the 59th Division. At 10.15 a.m. the Brigadier General addressed the Battalion, expressed his sorrow at our leaving. His Brigade wished us luck where we were going. At 10-30 a.m. the Battalion marched out of ARRAS to No 4 Camp at BLAIRVILLE. The bands from the other Battalions in the Bde. played us out. We reached BLAIRVILLE about 2 p.m. No men fell out on the march. We now belong to the 59th "A" Divn.	
BLAIRVILLE	22nd		The morning was spent in Games & foot inspections etc. A party of Officers N.C.O. were busy all day making a reconnaissance of the new areas in which the battalion will find work. This area was behind BULLECOURT.	
MORY	23rd		The Battalion left BLAIRVILLE today & marched to TUNNELLERS CAMP, MORY. 'B' Company took over Cures in ECOUST and C' billets in ST LEGER. I now fell out on the march.	

Army Form C. 2118.

WAR DIARY
or
INTELLIGENCE SUMMARY.
(Erase heading not required.)

Place	Date	Hour	Summary of Events and Information	Remarks and references to Appendices
MORY	February 24th		Today our first drafts as Pioneer Battalion began. Part of our men were out all day working on roads, repairing & clearing them. Another party were up at the trenches digging, laying wire-bonds etc. & at night the bigger party of all were up wiring both in the front & back system. All our orders come straight from the V.O.R.E. 59th Division.	
	25th		The parties went back for the roads for the uptake of the trenches were out during the day & the wiring parties were out as night. Today we have received orders from Division that in future a Pioneer Battalion will only consist of three Companies & the C.O. has decided that 'D' Coy. be divided up amongst 'A', 'B', 'C' Companies, a proportion of 'D' Coy. officers & men going to each. 'D' Company was broken up — 'B' joining 'B' Coy. at ECOUST, 'C' joining 'C' Coy. at ST LEGER & the remainder joining 'A' Coy. in TUNNELLERS CAMP, MORY.	
	26th		Today the usual work went on but at 2.30 pm D Coy officers going to each Coys of three Companies 'A','B','C'. The wiring parties went out as night.	
	27th		The parties on trench maintenance were out during the day & the wiring parties were out as usual at night. The men are becoming very good at the wiring now which is all of the double apron fence type. Part of 'A' Coy. 'Mori transport were bathed today & the rest of the Battalion Forestry Clean Clothing.	

WAR DIARY
or
INTELLIGENCE SUMMARY.

Army Form C. 2118.

Place	Date	Hour	Summary of Events and Information	Remarks and references to Appendices
MORY	February 28		The usual parties were out during the day working on the roads and cleaning up & lump-holing the trenches. The wiring parties were out at night. It is becoming darker during the early part of the night: however the wiring parties have now begun work until the moon comes out. The wires frog up from TUNNELLERS CAMP take about 2 after nine. We are going to try to get them taken up in future on lorries to-wards our the light Railway.	

J.M. Mum Lieut. Col.
commag.
6/7 Bn. Royal Scots Fusiliers.

59th Divisional Troops

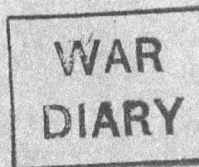

6/7th BATTALION

ROYAL SCOTS FUSILIERS

Pioneers

MARCH 1 9 1 8.

WAR DIARY
6/7 R.Sc.Fus. [Pi.]
MARCH 1918

𝄞 A LETTER FROM THE C.O.

CONFIDENTIAL.

WAR DIARY

6/7 ROYAL SCOTS FUSILIERS (PIONEERS)

from 1-3-18. to 31-3-18.

(Vol. XXII.)

WAR DIARY or INTELLIGENCE SUMMARY

Army Form C. 2118.

Place	Date March	Hour	Summary of Events and Information	Remarks and references to Appendices
MORY	1		The Battalion Headquarters are still at TUNNELLERS CAMP, MORY, 2 platoons of 'B' company at ECOUST and 'C' company at ST LEGER. During the day we have parties working on trench maintenance and on the repairing of HOMME-MORT - ECOUST road, SUCERIE - ECOUST road, and SUCERIE - VRAUCOURT road. During the night the remainder of the men are wiring and renewing barbed wire thrown out of the trenches during the day, so acts kind of 3' term. Last night we put up 1585 yards of wire. One wiring party got a salvo of phosphorus shells amongst them and 12 men were gassed and were sent to hospital.	
	2.		Today 'B' company moved into TUNNELLERS CAMP beside Headquarters, their billets at ST LEGER having been taken over by a company of the 34th Divisional Pioneer battalion. The usual parties were out during the day, and wiring was continued at night - 1540 yards being put up. From today the band are working a 'half-day shift' on the roads. 8 of our refugees let us to take up duty with the 59th Division.	
	3.		There were very few men on Church parade this morning as most of the men were out all night and were not up in time for them. The usual working parties were out, 900 yards of wire being put out that night. We have been given a plot of ½ an acre beside the camp to be cultivated by us - Lieutenant R. LEE has been appointed Battalion Agricultural Officer and has been out this morning to settle the ground prepared for seed.	

WAR DIARY
or
INTELLIGENCE SUMMARY.
(Erase heading not required.)

Army Form C. 2118.

Instructions regarding War Diaries and Intelligence Summaries are contained in F.S. Regs., Part II. and the Staff Manual respectively. Title pages will be prepared in manuscript.

Place	Date March	Hour	Summary of Events and Information	Remarks and references to Appendices
MORY	4.		The usual working parties were out today. 1800 yards of wire was put out last night. We relieved a letter today from the 47th Corps Heavy Artillery thanking us for the excellent work we had done for them last month prior to our leaving the 15th Division.	
	5.		The usual work has gone on today. Last night we put up 2090 yards of wire.	
	6.		The usual working parties were out. 2010 yards of wire were put up last night. Three of our officers have been away all afternoon attending a lecture at the VI Corps School on the Construction of Tunnel dug-outs.	
	7.		The usual work went on today. 2100x of wire put up. The transport year has had a special work party building barricade & round the Rhines in case of shell fire.	
	8.		The usual work went on – 2000x of wire were put up. Lieut. G.A. MASSIE was posted to 'B' Company for duty and Lieut. R.W. HOWATT was appointed acting Adjutant in his place.	
	9.		2 Platoons of 'A' Company relieved the 2 platoons of 'B' Company at ECOUST today but the Company H.Q. of 'A' Company remained in TUNNELLERS CAMP. The usual work went on – 1800 x of wire being put up. In addition 'B' 160 x were out, & a free air & sand for the Library were of the Battle system Odn were available today.	

Army Form C. 2118.

WAR DIARY
or
INTELLIGENCE SUMMARY.
(Erase heading not required.)

Instructions regarding War Diaries and Intelligence Summaries are contained in F.S. Regs., Part II. and the Staff Manual respectively. Title pages will be prepared in manuscript.

Place	Date March	Hour	Summary of Events and Information	Remarks and references to Appendices
MORY	10		Church services were held today but very few were on parade. The usual work went on — 1800× of wiring being done. At 11 p.m. last night all clocks were put forward 1 hour. — Summer time being brought into use.	
	11.		The usual work went on today. 1800× ft were put up last night. One forenoon at 10.15 a high velocity gun fired 10 shells on the camp at intervals of 4 minutes. We had no casualties.	
	12.		The usual work went on today. 2525× of wire were put up last night. All this wiring is now being done on the trench system. Tonight we received word that the enemy were likely to attack at dawn on the morning of the 13th. All night our guns sent over harassing fire on the enemy lines. One forenoon 10 shells were again dropped in the camp — We had no casualties.	
	13		The whole Battalion stood to as 5 a.m. this morning but all about down as soon as it was light as there was no signs of an enemy attack. The working parties during the day did not go out but the usual parties went out at night and 1475× of wire were put up. At 10 o'clock the all men in the camp were turned out for exercise in anticipation of the repetition of the shelling we had on the two previous days.	

Army Form C. 2118.

WAR DIARY
or
INTELLIGENCE SUMMARY.
(Erase heading not required.)

Place	Date March	Hour	Summary of Events and Information	Remarks and references to Appendices
MORY	14		The whole Battalion stood to at 5 a.m. From this morning schools down as soon as it was light. The artillery were firing harassing fire in the enemy front line & communication trenches all night – The usual working parties were out	
	15		The Battalion did not stand to at 5 a.m. this morning but the I. Officer received orders that each morning he had to got out at 5 a.m. & ascertain if the situation was normal. If anything unusual occurred he had orders to notify the Commanding Officer at once. The usual working parties were out. All the work at present was done on the support line of the Bama System – deepening is to 3 feet by 7 feet across the top.	
	16		The situation in front was unchanged. The usual digging parties were out working on the support line running behind ECOUST VILLAGE – The trench was dug to a depth of 18" along the whole of the Storvenne & hence four parties were digging it to a depth of 3'. On an average 600' were dug each night. The Battalion paraded at 12 noon today Kathersen Church Service in the	
THEATRE MORY.	17.		Battalion. After the service the Commanding Officer inspected the Battalion. At night the usual digging parties were out working on the assault trench. The digging is to be finished by Thursday.	

WAR DIARY
or
INTELLIGENCE SUMMARY.

Army Form C. 2118.

Place	Date	Hour	Summary of Events and Information	Remarks and references to Appendices
MORY.	MARCH 18.		Everything is still normal in front but the guard have been issued with special orders regarding what to do should anything the least bit unusual occur. All sentries have been instructed to be extremely vigilant. Today 250 of the men were allowed baths at MORY. The usual digging parties were out at night.	
	19.		Situation still unchanged. The usual working parties were out digging at night. In the afternoon today the men of the Battalion gave a concert in the THEATRE at MORY.	
	20.		Situation still unchanged. Every Officer & man in the Battalion including the Commanding Officer & adjutant went up to dig a fast on the support line & the Bomb System. This was done as an example by the Officers to the men and also to hurry on the important digging of the support trench. During the digging everything was extremely quiet, there was no enemy shelling at all. Everyone was back in camp by 12.30 a.m. having completed their 4 hours work.	
	21.		This morning the Battalion stood to at 5.30 a.m. and the Commanding Officer interviewed all Company Commanders as to the course to be taken should the Battalion be called upon to go into the line. Communication was kept up with the Half Company at ECOUST as long as possible - Drillers	

WAR DIARY or INTELLIGENCE SUMMARY

Army Form C. 2118.

Place	Date	Hour	Summary of Events and Information	Remarks and references to Appendices
MORY	March 21st (contd.)		Arrived at 1.15 p.m. instructing the Battalion to take up position at NOREUIL SWITCH. These were actually dug. The Battalion moved off at 2 p.m. At 3.30 p.m. the C.O. reported the Battalion holding the line from CEMETERY in front of VRAUCOURT to 500 yards left but not yet in touch on the flanks. About 4.10 p.m. enemy bom. reported coming in waves across crest line at C17C. Lewis and Machine gun fire was brought to bear on them and the Artillery was notified. Battalion H.Q. were established at SUCRERIE-VRAUCOURT road, an approximate tracing being sent to Brigade showing our position. Our right flank was now in touch with 7th BUFFS: left not yet in touch. The right flank of the Lincolns, who were on our left, was thrown back about this time but the managers to link up later although the enemy were really reinforcing. About 5 p.m. it was reported that the enemy had occupied VRAUCOURT COPSE. From landing small patrols up the valley. These patrols were held up by our snipers but not before they had captured our positions & signalled such to their Artillery by very lights. At 5.18 p.m. our heavy Artillery was firing about 500+ short, shells landing 70+ behind our front line. A message was sent hereifying this. At 5.30 p.m. the enemy appeared to be digging in about 400+ in front were however	

A 5834 W⁴ W 4973/M637 750,000 8/16 D.D.&L.Ltd. Forms/C.2118/13.

Army Form C. 2118.

WAR DIARY
or
INTELLIGENCE SUMMARY.
(Erase heading not required.)

Place	Date	Hour	Summary of Events and Information	Remarks and references to Appendices
VRAUCOURT (CONTIN.)	March 21		Scouts steered but had very few casualties concerning the amount of shell fire. We had again lost touch on our right flank so Major WILKIE went forward to make a reconnaissance and to try and find someone to link up with us on the right. After he had gone about 2000 yards Major WILKIE got into touch with the 8th BORDER REGIMENT, 25th DIVISION, 75 BRIGADE who had come through VAUX from ACHIET-LE-GRAND at 11 a.m. and who had taken up a position in front of VAUX with three companys in front and one in reserve. He got them to move down towards them left where they too gradually got in touch with our right flank. About 6 p.m. Major WILKIE reported that we were now in touch with the 8th BORDER REGIMENT on our right on the VAUX-SUCERIE ROAD. At 6 p.m. the above reconnaissance was reported	

WAR DIARY or INTELLIGENCE SUMMARY

Army Form C. 2118.

Place	Date March	Hour	Summary of Events and Information	Remarks and references to Appendices
VRAUCOURT	(contin) 21st		to the 177th Infantry Brigade. At 6 p.m. Captain DIXON, Commander of 'C' Company was wounded. Lieut Brews took charge of 'C' Company. At 6.35 p.m. Brigade sent orders to hang on to present line until reinforcements were being sent up. About 7.5 p.m. O.C. 'C' Coy sent word that enemy were pressing hard on our right & that they needed support. The 14th H.L.I. were in support at this point. At the same time 2/Lieut ROBERTSON reported wounded & also that the enemy were moving towards us in small parties. Fire was engaged by Vickers Guns, Lewis guns & rifle fire. As 9.22 p.m. both our flanks were in touch & the men were digging in. At 11.30 p.m. O.C. 'C' Coy. reported the capture of a machine gun & 7 prisoner.	
VRAUCOURT	22nd		Today at 12.25 a.m. Bde. Operation Order No 101 was received relieve and moving of Head Quarters. At 7.45 a.m. the C.O. reported to 177 Inf. Bde. that the Battalion was still holding position consolidated last night. & 20.C.7.6. to Cop.7.8. (VAUX-VRAUCOURT SHEET). At 9.30 a.m. 3 Lewis guns & 64 pans were received from Div. H.Q. where they had been left in A.A. positions. These were sent forward at once. O.C. 'B' Company reported our Lion 18 pounders falling short & a message was sent to Anzac Range Group. O.C. 'B' Coy. reported that	

WAR DIARY or INTELLIGENCE SUMMARY

Army Form C. 2118.

Place	Date	Hour	Summary of Events and Information	Remarks and references to Appendices
VRAUCOURT	MARCH 22 (CONTIN.)		2nd Lieut MUIR had been wounded. At 11-40 a.m. Companys were informed that the Battalion might be required to withdraw to the Army line to dig. At 12 noon O.C. "C" Coy. reported their 2/Lieut GODDING had been killed and that 2/Lieut SHERRIFF had been wounded. At 12.5 p.m. Headquarter Company moved to take up a defensive position in VAUX-VRAUCOURT under the Commanding Officer. Two strong points were formed and remainder were in Reserve. Great activity on part of enemy aircraft. At 1-25 p.m. O.C. "B" Coy. reported enemy coming over ridge in B21 in masses, our barrages being very effective enemy quickly dispersed. Brigade informed us that we are now under the orders of the 40th Division. At 1-40 p.m. C.O. reported to 119th Inf. Bde. that as enemy were again attacking it was imperative to withdraw meantime. At 3-30 p.m. Battalion prepared to withdraw to ECOUST-BAPAUME ROAD – O.C. Headquarters Coy. formed strong point to cover withdrawal. At 3-45 p.m. "A" Coy. were given orders to form a strong point in rear of VRAUCOURT to relieve H.Q. Coy. as soon as it was in position. At 3.50 p.m. the Battalion withdrew to the ECOUST-BAPAUME ROAD. At 4-15 p.m. the Battalion reached the road & dug in on the EAST side of it. 119th Inf Bde. of their new position. At 4-45 p.m. Captain HUTCHISON was reported killed by a sniper. Word was also	

WAR DIARY
or
INTELLIGENCE SUMMARY.
(Erase heading not required.)

Army Form C. 2118.

Place	Date MARCH	Hour	Summary of Events and Information	Remarks and references to Appendices
VRAUCOURT (CONTIN)	22.		received that the Enemy had occupied VRAUCOURT. At 5.55pm. O.C. Coys. were ordered to retire by echelons behind army wire. At 7.50 p.m. the Battalion consolidated behind Army Corps line. Bde. notified.	
	23.		At 8.5 a.m. this morning Lieut. Col. HART D.S.O. was wounded and Major WILKIE assumed command. This was notified to Brigade. During the day the Battalion was subjected to heavy bombardment but was able to keep the line intact. Any movement on the part of the Enemy was immediately stopped by Machine gun & Lewis gun fire	
BEHAGNIES	24.		This morning at 2.30 a.m. the Battalion was relieved by the 14th H.L.I. & 14th A. & S.H. Closing from right left the Battalion withdrew independently to a trench in rear of BEHAGNIES. This position was held all day although very heavily shelled. At 10.10 p.m. the Battalion vacated this trench & reached BOUCQUOY about 4 a.m.	
BOUCQUOY	25.		The Battalion stood to arms here until daylight.	
	26.		At 8 a.m. the Battalion rested in BOUCQUOY all day today. there was detailed as a flank guard to the 19th Division. left BOUCQUOY for FONQUEVILLERS on arrival At 6 p.m.	

Army Form C. 2118.

WAR DIARY
or
INTELLIGENCE SUMMARY.
(Erase heading not required.)

Place	Date March	Hour	Summary of Events and Information	Remarks and references to Appendices
BIENVILLERS	(contin) 26		the Battalion marched to BIENVILLERS where they were billeted for the night.	
SUS ST-LEGER	27.		At 8.15 am today the Battalion left BIENVILLERS for SUS-ST-LEGER where they were billeted.	
	28.		Rested in billets all day today.	
	29.		At 7pm this evening the Battalion moved to FREVENT where it entrained for HOUDAIN.	
HOUDAIN	30.		The Battalion detrained today at HOUDAIN at 2 a.m. went into billets there.	
	31.		During the Battalion rested in billets in HOUDAIN.	

Domville Lieut. Col.
Commdg.
6/7 Bn. Royal Scots Fusiliers (P)

31/3/18.

Telephone: 3083 } CITY.
3084

HISTORICAL SECTION (MILITARY BRANCH),
COMMITTEE OF IMPERIAL DEFENCE,
AUDIT HOUSE,
VICTORIA EMBANKMENT,
E.C.4.

22nd March

from Lt.Col.D.M.Wilkie,T.D. (late comdg.6/7 R.Sc.Fus.(Pi)
Clydesdale Bank House
Irvine
Ayrshire N.B.

Copy of a letter dated 19 Jan.

This diary was
returned 20.1.26

"...My Coy.Commander gave me his diary(wh.I enclose for perusal & return) which proves that we were continually in the front line.
    At dawn on 22nd Mar. our line roughly was from r.to l.,C 20,c,7,6,to C 19,b,7,8, There were no Br.troops in front of us;14th A & S.H. were continuing the line on our left and right. We held on to this position until 3 o'cl.when ordered to retire. HQ coy and A Coy(less 2 platoons wh had been captured the previous day near Ecoust)covered the retirement from about C 19,d,9,5,about 3.45 p.m. It was reported the enemy were in Vraucourt C,25,b,9,2 and we had to make a protecting flank with the 2 platoons of A Coy about B 30,b,2,9. These 2 platoons suffered heavy casualties losing their coy.comdr.killed. The 2 companies had now effected their retirement to Ecoust-Bapaume Rd and immediately they began consolidating the position at B 30,c. Ultimately we were ordered to retire to the partly dug Army Line about B 29,a,& b and began at once to consolidat the position. My HQ were at B,29,a,1,1. We held on to this position unti relieved a.m.24th at 2.30 by H.L.I.& A & S.H.closing from l.to r. We afterwards took up a fresh position in a trench in rear of Behagnies. It was afterwards commented that because of the devotion to duty of the 6/7 R Sc.Fus on 21st Mar.they undoubtedly held up the German advance at a very critical time,but owing to their coming under the command of several administrations they did not get their due credit.

They got a special chit from
Gen. ROMER
L.W?

Extract from War Diary for March 1918
6/7 Royal Scots Fuslrs.(Pioneers)

Vraucourt. 22nd. Today at 12.25 a.m. Bde. operation order no.101 was received reliefs and moving of Headquarters. At 7.45 a.m. the C.O. reported to 177th Inf. Bde. that the battalion was still holding position consolidated last night C.20.c.7.6. to C.19.b.7.8.. At 9.30 a.m. 3 Lewis Guns and 64 pans were received from Divl.H.Q. where they had been in A.A.positions. These were sent forward at once. O.C.B.Coy. reported our own 18-pdrs. falling short & a message was sent back to have range lengthened. At 9.50 a.m. O.C.B. Coy. reported that 2/Lt Muir had been wounded. At 11.40 a.m. Coys. were informed that the Bn. might be required to withdraw to the Army Line to dig in...... At 12.5 p.m. HQ Coy. moved to take up a defensive position in ~~Ymla~~ Vraucourt under the Comdg. Offr. Two strong points were formed and the remainder were in reserve.....
At 1.25 p.m. O.C.B.Coy. reported enemy coming over ridge in C.21 in masses, our barrage being very effective enemy quickly dispersed. Bde. informed us that we are now under orders of 40th Div. At 1.40 p.m. C.O. reported to 177 Bde that as enemy were again attacking it was impossible to withdraw meantime. At 3.50 p.m. Bn. prepared to withdraw to Ecoust-Bapaume road - O.C.HQ.Coy. formed strong point A.Coy. were given orders to form a strong point in rear of Vraucourt & relieve H.Q.Coy. as soon as it was in position. At 3.50 pm to cover withdrawal. At 3.45 p.m. the Bn. withdrew to the Ecoust-Bapaume road. At 4.15 p.m. the Bn. reached the road and dug in on the East side of it & informed bde. of their new position. At 4.15 p.m..... was word also received that enemy had occupied Vraucourt. At 5.55 p.m. O.C.Coys. were ordered to retire by sections behind army wire. At 7.50 p.m. the battalion consolidated behind Army Line - Bde. notified.

23rd. At 8.5.am.... Major Wilkie assumed command. During the day the battalion.... was able to keep the line intact

Behagnies. 24th. This morning at 2.30 a.m. the Battn. was relieved by the 14th H.L.I. & 14 A.& S.H. closing from right and left and the Battn. withdrew independently to a trench in rear of Behagnies.....

SCALE 1:40,000.

BATTLE ZONE

3RD SYSTEM   2ND SYSTEM

FRONT LINE.
A.M.
21st MAR

Br. FRONT LINE DAWN 22ND

BRITISH FRONT LINE DAWN 23RD

59th Divisional Pioneers

6/7th BATTALION

ROYAL SCOTS FUSILIERS (Pioneers)

APRIL 1918.

WAR DIARY
or
INTELLIGENCE SUMMARY.

Army Form C. 2118.

23B
y shown

Place	Date	Hour	Summary of Events and Information	Remarks and references to Appendices
HOUDAIN	Sept. 1		The Battalion left HOUDAIN at 12 noon by train for PROVEN arrival station. Key arrived about 7 p.m. from PROVEN STATION we marched to SCHOOL CAMP, WATOU, and remained there for the night.	
WATOU	2		Remained at SCHOOL CAMP all day. All men are now being re-equipped and prepared for the line again. Draft of 22 arrived from Base still in SCHOOL CAMP. At 8 A.M. a reconnoitring party of Officers and N.C.Os left by bus to go over the forward area EAST of YPRES with representatives of 18th MIDDLESEX Regt of Pioneers whom we are to relieve to-morrow. In the afternoon the 177 Inf Bde and our Battalion were inspected by the Army Commander who addressed all officers after the inspection. In the evening another draft of 20 arrived from the Base.	
	3	10.30 A.M.	At 10.30 A.M. we left SCHOOL CAMP and marched to QUINTON STATION, PAPERINGHE, where we entrained on the light railway for MIDDLESEX CAMP. We arrived about 2 p.m. & took over the camp from 18th MIDDLESEX REGT (P).	
MIDDLESEX CAMP. YPRES.	4	4.30 A.M.	At 4.30 A.M. we sent out working parties to work on posts which were being built in Reserve Line. Other parties were detailed to patrol all forward tracks and roads in the Divisional area & to keep them in repair. Other parties were taken up the light railway from MANNERS JUNCTION at 5 A.M. & brought back by a train reaching camp at 2 p.m. Other parties remained in camp to work on its general improvement that has been a lot of rain to-day and the ground is in a very heavy condition.	
	5			

WAR DIARY or INTELLIGENCE SUMMARY

Army Form C. 2118.

Place	Date	Hour	Summary of Events and Information	Remarks and references to Appendices
MIDD-ESEX CAMP YPRES	April 6		The same working parties went out to-day. The ground is very bad round the post in which they are working & it is slow work building up the breast-works. More rain has fallen.	
"	7		The usual working parties went out to-day. The weather is much milder and orders have been issued that men in camp must stay inside ever as much as possible as hostile balloons are up. About 2.30 p.m. an E.A. came overhead flying high but was driven off by A.A. fire.	
"	8		The usual parties went out working to-day. During the evening hostile artillery was active on back areas but no shells burst over the camp. All men with the Battalion have now been re-equipped.	
"	9		The usual working parties went out. It was found that the tracks had been broken in a good many places by hostile shelling on the previous night. These were all repaired. If shas been very quiet to-day and the artillery was quiet until about 11 p.m. when there was much activity on both sides. This kept up all night.	
"	10		Order received from 59" Bge to hold one company (13 Coy in readiness to former Army Battle Zone & attached to 0 under orders of O.C. 2/5- LINCOLNS, remainder of Battalion to be in Divisional Reserve at disposal of G.O.C. French Ref & extra ammunition were issued. The camp was shelled during evening. Working parties were out as usual.	

Army Form C. 2118.

WAR DIARY or INTELLIGENCE SUMMARY

Army Form C. 2118.

Place	Date	Hour	Summary of Events and Information	Remarks and references to Appendices
MIDDLESEX CAMP YPRES	April 11.		All ranks "Stood to" at 5 A.M. at 6 o'clock from camp was again shelled. The shelling lasting about 2 hours. The Orderly Room received a direct hit. Asst. Adjutant Capt. Shimocks & Serjeant O.R. being wounded & 1 O.R. killed. The usual working parties went out as on other days.	
"	12.		The same working parties went out to day. Orders from 57 Division was received to get everything ready to move at 1 p.m. MIDDLESEX CAMP was evacuated. Battalion detrained at BRANDHOEK & marched direct to WARRINGTON CAMP.	
"	13.		VLAMERTINGHE AREA arriving there at 5.30 A.M. & left BRANDHOEK by train at 1.45 p.m. detraining at GODEWAERSVELDE where we marched to BERTHEN where we bivouacked for the night.	
"	14.		Battalion "Stood to" at 5 A.M. at BERTHEN at 10 A.M. & killed at WESTOUTRE. When instructions were received to concentrate at WINDMILL MONT ROUGE in LOCRE area. Orders were received to reconnoitre MTEEREN - DRANOUTRE line as it was probable we would be required to take it over from 34 Division. Same night the Battalion was meeting off at 11.30 p.m. An order was received to turn & concentrate in WESTOUTRE area.	
"	15		Battalion arrived at ONTARIO CAMP, S. of RENINGHELST about 3 A.M. & marched at 10 A.M. to CROIX DE POPERINGHE. B & C Coys were sent as recce to 176 Inf. Bde., occupying army line from S.8.b.6.6 to S.3.d.7.4. (Sheet 28). About 6.30 p.m., B Coy reported holding Army line then on Hill 75 & B Coy under observation. C & B Coy considered they were not strong enough to hold & asked for support to counter attack. This was reported to 176 Bde. At 7.20 p.m. order from 59 Div. to place 2 companies under command of 177 Inf. Bde. & to "Stand to" all ranks to H.Q. 177 Bde. for instructions.	

WAR DIARY or INTELLIGENCE SUMMARY

Army Form C. 2118.

Place	Date	Hour	Summary of Events and Information	Remarks and references to Appendices
	April 15 (cont'd)	At 8 p.m.	2/Lt both B Coy reported "Most collected about 500 stragglers of 176 Bde & made them hold "Army line" behind BAILLEUL. In touch on left flank of Bn patrol reports enemy about MDX S.E. of BAILLEUL.	
	16.	At 12.30 a.m.	orders received to concentrate at LOCRE & reorganise. Survivors being in Corps Reserve. Battalion was placed under orders of B/Gen James for counter-attack & were ordered to concentrate about M.29 a 5.4. 469 Coy R.E. coming under orders D.C. O/C Royal Scots Fusiliers. At 5.40 p.m. Battalion dug in at place ordered, but received instructions to return to LOCRE at midnight. Companies ordered to return to assault positions at M.29 by 8 a.m. At 8.30 a.m. 100 rifles of 'A' Coy placed at disposal of 100 Inf. Bde. for counter-attack if necessary. Patrols sent out each hour. At 12.25 p.m. 2/Lt D.S. McDonald sent to replace 2/Lt O'Quillan (wounded) in charge of 100 rifles above mentioned. At 1 p.m. 2/Lt. Fleming was sent to reconnoitre vicinity of N.25 Central with a Lincoln S.P.E. officer. At 4 p.m. orders received "Be prepared to move your command (less Coy detached) to M.34 a 3 be under orders of 146 Inf Bde. At 6 p.m. a further order placed Battalion under orders of 177 Inf Bde. the Battalion was in position selected.	
		At 11.45 p.m.		
	17.	At 1 a.m.	Survivors of 100 rifles detached for counter-attack reported at Bn. H.Q. they had made an attack suffering 20 casualties including 2/Lt McDonald (since died of wounds). At 6 a.m. 13 Coy reported "French to our immediate front relieved by Battalion which counter-attacked last night - no one on their flanks. Own morning 2 platoons of 13 Coy to occupy trench on Left. R.E. Coy reported Y & L front & SHERWOOD Fors on Rgt. At 12 noon Bn.H.Q. moved to LOCRE CHATEAU General situation now quiet.	
	18.			

WAR DIARY
or
INTELLIGENCE SUMMARY.
(Erase heading not required.)

Army Form C. 2118.

Place	Date	Hour	Summary of Events and Information	Remarks and references to Appendices
	April 19		Situation at 6 a.m. normal – Casualties light. At 2.45 a.m. Battalion was advised that 49th Division would be relieved by 34th French Division that night. All arrangements were made for guides etc. and at 6 p.m. Batt. received orders to Concentrate at RENINGHELST, billets being reached about midnight. Three Officers & three runners were left at LOCRE CHATEAU at disposal of French Batt. H. Qrs. (Battalion).	
	20		At 2 p.m. Battalion proceeded by march route to DIRTY BUCKET CAMP A.19.c sheet 28. On arrival there received further orders to march to STRETFORD CAMP A.3.c.1.7 (sheet 28) where they spent the night. Battalion proceeded to HOUTKERQUE by march route where the greatest difficulty was experienced in procuring billets. B Coy having the greatest.	
HOUTKERQUE	21		Day spent in arranging billets, cleaning & re-equipping.	
	22		A Coy. employed preparing defensive positions in neighbourhood of WATOU, B & C Coys drilling & Cleaning	
	23		Work on defensive positions carried on by A Coy. Same work carried on by B & C Coys.	
	24		Working parties as usual	
	25			
	26			
	27		After working on nearby Road all day the Battalion marched at 10 p.m. to ST JAN TER BIEZEN where they bivouaced for the night no billets being available. Battalion remained at ST JAN TER BIEZEN shelter being procured for the night, marched to neighbourhood S of POPERINGHE. H.Q. at farm at L.34.a.5.6.	
	28			
	29		Battalion (sheet 27). 1 Coy dug hastily round & put into a state of defence 3 farms. The other two Coys in neighbourhood of RENINGHELT	

Army Form C. 2118.

WAR DIARY
or
INTELLIGENCE SUMMARY.
(Erase heading not required.)

Place	Date	Hour	Summary of Events and Information	Remarks and references to Appendices
	April 30		250 men were engaged in digging from S.31.b.1.7 (sheet 28) digging reserve line from L.35.d.2.5 (sheet 27) and 250 men	

J. M. Fal Rice
Lt. Col.
Comdg. 2/1 N.W. Fus 2/1

CONFIDENTIAL

6/7 RSF

WAR DIARY

6/7th Royal Scots Fusiliers — (Pioneers)

From 1-5-18.   To 31-5-18.

(Vol. XXIV)

WAR DIARY or INTELLIGENCE SUMMARY

Army Form C. 2118.

Vol 36

24 G
5 sheets

Place	Date	Hour	Summary of Events and Information	Remarks and references to Appendices
Farm L.30.a.5.6. (Sheet 27)	May 1.		The whole Battalion (i.e. 3 Companies) engaged in completion of Switch line (Q.32, G.B.2 — GOES MOET HILL, G.30.6.9.4), B Coy. digging gaps and A & C Coys wiring. Lieut F.A MOORE and 2/Lieut T. SHARP granted permission to wear badges of rank of Captain, pending appearance in Gazette, whilst in command of Capt. SHELLEY in neighbourhood of Farm.	
— do —	2.		One Coy engaged wiring part of the Switch line dug out the previous day, the other two Coys digging reserve line to this Switch line. The work on several occasions been hindered by shortage of wiring material & the distance of Dumps from which material could be drawn.	
— do —	3.		A Coy. engaged wiring line dug by 33rd Sqs. from L.35.d.1.4 (sheet 27) B & C Coys dug 4820 feet of trench from L.34.b.1.2 (S. of)	
— do —	4.		No issue being available all 3 Coys engaged digging from R.2.8.2.9 (S.27) Eastwards & Bent north. Proceeded to join 1st Bn. Royal Scots Fus. (Authy A.G./2158/22440(0) of 28/4/18) at request of A. Gd. E.D.S. Gordon, famille C.O. of this unit.	
— do —	5.		2 Coys. wiring 3200x stating at L.35.d.2.6 (sheet 27), the remaining Coy. digging reserve line from K.36.d.1.6 (sheet 27)	
HOUTKERQUE E.20.b (L.7)	6.		The same working parties out to-day with instructions to proceed on completion of task to HOUTKERQUE where Battalion was housed in tents at SHRINE CAMP? by 6 p.m. Orders received that Battalion would proceed on 7th inst. to ST. MOMELIN.	
ST. OMER	7		Battalion entrained at 8 a.m. proceeding by HOUTKERQUE — HERZEELE — WYLDER — WORMHOUDT — ZEGERS CAPEL to ST. MOMELIN, and thence by road route to ST. OMER no billets being procurable at former place. Battalion billeted in Barracks, & necessary orders were issued for relieving the Battalion to a Battalion Training Cadre (Authy 59 Div. C./269/A d/5-5-18).	
— do —	8.		13 Officers and 678 O.R. sent to M Section Base Depot, CALAIS. Before departure Battalion was	

WAR DIARY
or
INTELLIGENCE SUMMARY.
(Erase heading not required.)

Army Form C. 2118.

Place	Date	Hour	Summary of Events and Information	Remarks and references to Appendices
ST. OMER.	May 8. (contd.)		paraded & addressed by Gen. Ramer G.O.C. 59th Div. Transport complete and Band to remain meaning the latter are arranged with A.Q.M.G. 55th Div.	
REBECQ.	9.		Day spent in making up Battalion rolls etc.	
	10.		Remainder of Battalion - now a Battalion Training Cadre - proceeded by march route to REBECQ where the night was spent. Batt. is now under orders of 176 Inf. Bde.	
NEDONCHELLE	11.		Battalion set out by march route for FIEFS but destination was changed en route by orders of 176 Inf. Bde. to NEDONCHELLE which was reached at 12 noon.	
— do —	12.		Surplus personnel - 9 O.R. - Sent to Base to-day. Capt. J. Watson & 2/Lieut. W.K. Farley returned from R.E. Comm ROUEN.	
— do —	13.		176 Inf. Bde. wire (repeated) states that this Battalion will be transferred to 177 Inf. Bde. on 14 inst.	
Estrée-Cauchie	14		The Battalion proceeded by march route to ESTREE - CAUCHIE via AMETTES - FERFAY - CAMBLAIN CHATELAIN - HOUDAIN - REGREUVE - ESTREE CAUCHIE route; good billeting arrangements having been made by Staff Captain 177th Bde.	
— do —	15.		The Commanding Officer and Coy. Commanders reconnoitered the B.B. Line from Q.21.a.9.9. — J.26.a.5.o. (sheet 36B) this sector is held by 11th Bn. Somerset Light Inf. In case of the enemy breaking through the 91st Royal Scots Then have orders to send out parties to collect stragglers & place them in the most suitable posts in this sector this reinforcing the line. Under 59th Divisional C/2109/A dated 5/5/18 the Regimental Pipes & Drummers and Transport (less 6 Riders, Hors Cart, Water Cart, 4 grooms and 7 drivers) proceeded to Etrat. Strength of Battalion as above. Bjwsarded to Etten.	

WAR DIARY or INTELLIGENCE SUMMARY

Army Form C. 2118.

Place	Date	Hour	Summary of Events and Information	Remarks and references to Appendices
ESTREE-CAUCHIE	May 16.		Roads leading into our Sector (C Sector) of B.B. Line were reconnoitred by Coy Commanders to-day and collecting points fixed. The Sector is divided into 3. A Coy right, B Coy centre and C Coy on the left.	
- do -	17		B.B. Line reconnoitred by Coy Commanders and scheme of work to N.C.Os.	
- do -	18.		Defence Scheme for B.B. Line prepared & forwarded to H.Q. 177 Inf. Bde.	
MAMETZ	19.		Under orders of 59 Division the Battalion proceeded by bus to MAMETZ	
- do -	20.		The Battalion Training Cadre now working under orders of C.R.E. of C. Seston (10th Corps) supervising Chinese on the B.B. Line, the officers & N.C.Os being spread over the various sub-sectors.	
- do -	21		Work proceeding as usual. 2/Capt. Pettigrew & Mr. Ireton returned from 6 months spell in U.K. & are proceeding to Base, being supernumerary to Establishment of a Training Cadre.	
- do -	22.		Same work proceeding. N.C.Os now filled beside their work.	
- do -	23			
- do -	24			
- do -	25			
- do -	26		Work proceeding on B.B. Line.	
- do -	27			
- do -	28			
- do -	29			
- do -	30			
- do -	31			

A. Winter
Lt. Col.
Comdg. 4/7 Royal Scots Fus (P.)

Headquarters
59th Divn. 'G'

With ref to your letter No. 329/2G
d/1/6/18. It is much regretted that
the original has been forwarded in
error to Officer i/c Records
Hamilton.

I have under the circumstances
returned the copy, but if you still
so desire to have original applic-
ation could be made to O i/c Records
Hamilton to have it returned.

General Staff stamp: No. 329/2G Date 1-6-17 59th (NORTH MIDLAND) DIVISION

Stamp: 6/7TH BATTALION, THE ROYAL SCOTS FUSILIERS. No. LJ4 318 Date 1/6/18

Rm Howatt Capt
a/adjutant
for OC 6/7th R.S.F. (D)

www.ingramcontent.com/pod-product-compliance
Lightning Source LLC
Chambersburg PA
CBHW081459160426
43193CB00013B/2539